The Poetrygram Annual 2020

Copyright © 2020 by Helen Cox.

Published in the United Kingdom by Helen Cox Books.

Paperback ISBN: 978-1-914238-40-6

Hardback ISBN: 978-1-914238-41-3

No part of this book may be used or reproduced in any manner whatsoever without written permission except in the case of brief quotations embodied in critical articles or reviews. Rights to the poems remain with the poets. Rights to all other materials enclosed remain with the editor, Helen Cox. For further information, visit helencoxbooks.com.

The Poetrygram Annual 2020

Edited by Helen Cox

TABLE OF CONTENTS

Introduction 6

Masked 9

Interview with the Poetrygram Prize Winner 2020: Greg Rowan Shearer 10

Tiny Pin Cushion Woman 13

Untitled 15

An Ethic of Encounter 16

Ghosts in the Corners 17

An Unwelcome Guest... 19

Slowing... 20

George Floyd... 21

When the Kissing Had to Stop 22

The Brock Path 25

How To Carry Grief 27

The New Normal... 28

Diamonds 30

Once Upon a Time in Lockdown 32

Equality Matters 34

Don't Touch Your Face 36

Regenerated Rings 38

Night Light 40

A Dionysian Swell 42

Whispers of the Soul 44

Left 46

Lockdown 48

What's Important Now – 2020 49

Poet Biographies 50

Introduction

As a long-time journaler (I've kept a journal on and off since I was about fifteen years old), I've understood the blank page to be a safe space for many years. Until 2020 however, I had no idea that so many other writers, artists and poets felt the same way. Which, if you think about it, is a little silly of me. But then those who know me will tell you I am prone to being more than a little silly at times. Because of course it stands to reason that if the blank page is a safe space for me, it is likely to be so for others. A place where one can express, explore, challenge, protest and riot uninterrupted.

This year, when all the coffee shops in Britain, and beyond, were ordered to shut down. When every gymnasium and art gallery closed its doors. When every favourite local pub and restaurant had to postpone service, writers still congregated. Safely and within the rules of the government's stringent anti-corona virus guidelines. Writers flocked to the page – whatever that looked like for them.

A word document. An Instagram post. An old notebook in the back of the drawer. And many readers also escaped into our stories, poems, essays and blogposts. In a way, that's what readers and writers have most in common. They both seek solace between the pages.

Why am I taking the time to labour this point? I promise there is an end game. And one decidedly more inspiring than anything I've seen come out of the Marvel universe of late.

Here it is.

Though we've been locked away physically, almost every artist I know has used the time to focus on creation. That's not to say they were lucky enough to sit down and write an epic novel or a collection of poetry – though some did. But in many cases, having absolutely no social life besides a weekly zoom meeting with family members gave the creative-minded space to stop, take stock, think, muse, plan and conspire.

Thus, although even as I write this the immediate future feels most uncertain, I think there is one grain of certainty we can cling to. In the post-vaccination universe (official term) we are going to see an explosion in artistic output. People will release the books, put on the plays, unveil the paintings, direct the movies, choreograph the ballets, sing the operas that have been formulated during this enforced period of isolation and reflection. I also suspect that due to the lengthy restrictions placed on our way of life, these creations are likely to be more daring and ground-breaking because, well, where else can we push boundaries right now without endangering our beloved and much-needed NHS?

Moreover, because we have spent such a considerable amount of time going without new creative output I suspect we are going to be amongst the most appreciative audiences in history.

Consequently, despite the general undercurrent of uncertainty, I choose to look to the year ahead with hope and excitement about what might be in the works at this very moment, even if we cannot see it happening directly, and invite you to do the same. Though nobody wants to live through a year like the one just gone I believe the artistic explosion on the horizon is going to be nothing short of dazzling. It will not bring back all we have lost. But it may serve to guide us into a different future.

Masked

I am not the highwaywoman disguised as a man so I can suck all the emeralds from your naked fingers. Or kiss the gasps from your lips because you have pined for the taste of an outlaw for as long as you can remember. I am not the caped hero who just found out Donald Trump is my real father, hiding my secret identity behind a flimsy visor and fooling my closest friends into believing I'm just another mild-mannered reporter, rather than a super girl with the strength to bench press helicopters. I am not the hot wife in a porno spread-eagled on an eiderdown I bought from the Martha Stewart website, a length of black silk tied across my eyes so my husband doesn't recognise me later when he strokes his cock to the spectacle of our neighbour fucking me in nothing but his unwashed sports socks. I am not the villain in a slasher flick, sparing the cheerleaders and stalking the high school's arrogant jocks in their scarlet letterman jackets, dreaming up infinite ways to stab them through the gut before scrawling the word 'slut' across a football pep rally banner in their own philandering blood.

I am an ice sculpture in the frozen section of my local grocery store.

A poet, masquerading in a medical mask I bought from K-Mart, wondering if there is an aisle in here that stocks Adventure. Or if they are all sold out until further notice.

Interview with the Poetrygram Prize Winner 2020:
Greg Rowan Shearer

Helen: The poem you submitted to this year's contest was deeply moving. What inspired that poem?

Greg: My mother inspired the poem. She's an inspirational person who has been through so much. She's a warrior dressed up as this little Glaswegian woman. We were coming out of a hospital appointment, she was holding my arm when we had to cross the road and I took her hand. When we reached the other side she laughed and said: 'God, I remember I used to hold your hand crossing the road when you were a little boy'. Suddenly, I realised that our roles had reversed and I felt this wave of emotion that eventually became the poem.

Helen: When did you first know or decide to become a poet?

Greg: I had written little things here and there for years but I had never really thought my work was worthwhile. I started an English and Creative Writing course on my journey to become an English teacher and one of the modules was concerned with poetry. A lecturer read my poems and told me I should try getting my poetry published or find a space to perform. I didn't think it would go anywhere (or that a working class guy from Glasgow would get to call himself a poet) but some people liked my poetry and places I performed kept asking me to come back.

Helen: What or who are your major influences as a poet?

Greg: Language is something that's really close to my heart. I've always loved language, writing and reading. I think my background has been an inspiration, growing up in Glasgow and sharing my life with the people I have. I also owe so much to my English teacher Brenda, she saved my life.

In terms of poets who have influenced me there's so many but I love Jackie Kay, Ocean Vuong, Danez Smith, Langston Hughes, Holly McNish, Jim Ferguson, my good pal Samuel Glover, Tom Leonard and the eminent Charles Bukowski.

Helen: 2020 has certainly been a year for the history books and lots of people have taken up creative writing in response to some of the strangeness we've all experienced. Why do you think poetry is so important to us in times of strain or uncertainty?

Greg: I think in times where we all feel so disconnected everyone just wants to be heard. That's the beauty of poetry, you are communicating a feeling or an emotion or a memory. It's like a chrysalis or a snapshot taken with words instead of a camera. During times like these people have so much emotion that they need to share and happily they are turning to poetry. It takes a lot of bravery to let someone read something so personal that you've crafted from your thoughts so I think in times like these it's heartening to know that people are finding their voices and getting braver.

Helen: What writing tips can you offer other poets? What's worked well for you?

Greg: The best advice I can give is to write something every day, even if it never sees the light of day. Even if it's a word or a sentence. If you don't work the writing muscle it will wither. You also need to be prepared to bare yourself in every piece of writing. It sounds romantic but writing is a painful process, the best pieces always reveal an aspect of yourself and sometimes it hurts but there's a catharsis to putting it all down on paper.

Helen: What poetry projects are you working on and where can people read your words?

Greg: I'm working on a chapbook at the moment and hopefully that will be out sometime in 2021. People can read my work on my Instagram page @grspoetry.

Tiny Pin Cushion Woman

O' tiny pin cushion woman,
patron saint of NHS surgeries,
I hold your hand as we cross the street.

Time's hands caress you
with fingertips of broken glass,
leave you like colouring book pages
in hospital waiting rooms.

You laugh sometimes saying
you ought to be Shelley's Eve,
bruised like a peach, cut like a lemon,
held together with costume jewellery,
tea with two Sweetex
and lust for life.

You have never been anything but beautiful
I have never known any different or better,
since long before the creep of age,
before the sickly stream of result letters,
before the cancer and the transplants,
before the surgeries and the suffrage,
before the sainthood,
and survival, still after,
you would never be any less than whole,

holy, wholly mine,
My Mum.

O' tiny pin cushion woman,
I miss like my own milk teeth the days,
when you held my hand as we crossed the street.

Greg Rowan Shearer

Untitled

I was going to start with
'When we meet again,'
but I realised
how trite that sounded.

Then I thought of,
'Next time we meet,'
but, let's be honest,
that's no better either.

The fact is
we don't know
when that'll be.
And the not knowing
is absolutely
the worst part of it all.

Katherine Fitton

An Ethic of Encounter

Syncopated steps
– tentative at first –
beneath the veneer
a yearning to entwine.

We could have set each other alight

but my duty is to resist...
while you seek an inlet
an unlocked door
a window left ajar

and yet, when you find a nook
you stand and stare
as if awaiting an invitation
knowing I cannot allow it.

It's almost as if this is the dance:

You: wondering if they were left open on purpose.
Me: wondering the same.

Heather Joy

Ghosts in the Corners

...ghosts, ghosts are crowding
the dark corners of recollection now
pale shadows that mouth wails of greeting
transparent, thin-voiced, desperate....

of course they don't see you, don't know you, they
are only metaphors of the nerves
no more than automatic memories
paraded round you by the tedious brain
to populate the darkness
no one there

the people that they were are different now
or dead, or lost within their own despairs
or happy in some new and quieter way
than you all, young, had once looked forward to

the mountain cottage and the garden patch
replaced by a city room near good cafés
for the unambitious lucky; a stately manor
now just a tract house on a cul-de-sac for others

for some the doorway and the ragged blanket
for some the gurney and the loud attendant

the ghosts of youth, so sentimental, have no say
in this future that is now
your now and so they wail and clamor to remind you
that yes you once were young and scorned the dark
who are now so pale that only darkness shows you

Richard Risemberg

An Unwelcome Guest

Back in mid-Winter, with a cold steady grip,
news spread from the East and was all about you.

In Spring you bounced in with a hop and a skip,
you were green, fresh and keen, how little we knew.

The Summer sun blazed and we gave you the slip
in pubs and on beaches your mingling grew.

Now heading to Autumn, as trees start to strip,
we wish that you'd go but you're sticking like glue.

Sharron Green

Slowing

Birds were no safer from roaming cats
yet they benefited from stark roads,
fewer wheels, fewer fumes, fewer moving things.

And goats moved into villages, free running
pavements and green spaces, gangs
on the rampage, claiming back what was theirs.

And sheep safely grazed on roadside verges,
nosed their way into parks, nothing
was barred from them.

And earth breathed without choking,
soil sung and waterways glistened and sprung
as the world slowed and found harmony again.

Heather Walker

George Floyd

So many feelings but nothing concrete
then my thoughts go back
to George Floyd in the street.

Cops knee on his neck
his actions were weak
he just took his life
and pressed delete.

Those 9 minutes of hell we were in disbelief
he cried, "I CAN'T BREATHE," and said it on repeat.

He called for his Momma
people looked on in defeat
we all watched in horror
while he died there in the street.

Tony Simms

When the Kissing Had to Stop

When the kissing had to stop
and the hand-shakes ceased
we began to bump the elbow –
often missing, with a laugh,

embarrassed, till we learnt to stand
apart, to avoid and separate
under orders from the floor –
those black and yellow waspish tapes

directing you to go one way
or worse, to stop.
Much waiting followed
in spaced-out queues

and so we all lost touch.
We could phone, email or zoom
sit down and write a letter –
but none of these was quite the same

even though we kept repeating
how nice to see and hear from you.
No, a voice is not enough
nor an image on a screen

we need to touch, and to be
touched ourselves. A pat or push,
nudge, friendly shove –
go on with you, was that really

what you meant? Perhaps it's time
to shake hands on it, make it real –
which is now prohibited.
Keep well away. Keep ill away.

Make sure you keep your distance.
Do not touch me, don't come close
do not even visit me.
They call it social distancing –

the distance makes it anti-social.
So, now cut off and out of touch
wanting even elbow contact
I should love to touch once more

old friends, acquaintances and children,
to give them all a hug –
to feel the press of human flesh
since the kissing had to stop.

Richard Westcott

The Brock Path

reveals
a forage
in the night
under the metal fence,
across the man-made ditch,
over the stone dyke.

Paw prints lead beyond
the boundaries we created –
leaving traces.

A single hair
caught on barbed wire
ducked beneath,
snuffled pits between
military rows of planted
deepening larches,

along ancient tracks
he did not make
but seems compelled

to follow.
Compelled to follow

I thought
the drive to seek exceeded powers of fright –
we were restricted

I felt
we were confined

but on reflection
it seems
everything
needs to be protected
by edges.

Annie Sturgeon

How To Carry Grief

be faithful to the grief
           let feet take instruction from ground
prepare to embrace ancestors

sing to bring them back
                    repair the rift
                  a sweetness of keening

let blessings land
           invite story into yourself
bequeath a narrative for seven generations from now

believe there will be an earth to sustain us   then

Scott-Patrick Mitchell

The New Normal

Locked in a moment of history
sealed in the amber archives
palm trees sway over Mar-A-Lago
the air is getting warm this time of year

tough guys tweet:
OBAMAGATE!!!

It goes away in April
just cough into your elbow
CDC says wear a mask
the President never wears one

The Ramp was like an ice-skating rink
The Phone Call was perfect

250,000+ US lives lost
Russians bounty off American soldiers
Washington "Redskins" to announce new moniker
but now how will Native Americans ever learn of their heritage?

The premier source for authentic Latino cuisine –
if it's Goya, it has to be hogwash

Demon Sperm
Alien DNA
I don't take responsibility at all

it is what it is
'Cheese Pizza' doesn't mean what you think it means
We Are Your Family Now

stand back
stand by
Forever Non-Essentially Yours
FUGERE CITO, LONGE, ET TARDE REVERT

Christian Garduno

Diamonds

Diamonds
are a girl's best friend,
they say, insurance for a rainy day
needed now more than ever
as she looks into the mirror
and the leathered face of
her old mother
stares right
back.

It's so
unfair, she thinks
life so full of promise then.
She was the belle of the ball
won leading roles in films;
she was a goddess.
But now alas
reduced
to this…

Husbands.
They come and go
nothing stays the same
'Til death us do part' became
Til you lose your looks,
Til the wrinkles show,
Til gravity has
claimed your
figure.

Diamonds
are forever.
She believes she sees
their sparkle reflected in her eyes,
still a tiny spark of eternity.
Glamour may be gone
but time can't quench
the fire in
her soul.

Jacqueline Fowle

Once Upon a Time in Lockdown

Monday evening,
hearts beat fast,
truth in rumours,
freedoms dashed.

Unclear instructions,
unexpected despair.
Distorted reality,
unimaginable repair.

Normality questioned,
moral all time low,
life is fragile,
lives put on hold.

One way systems,
supermarket wars.
Disinfect our lives,
sanitise our thoughts.

A hidden assassin,
a future unknown.
Economic breakdown,
high risk zones.

Be socially distant,
please wear a mask,
must stay alert,
this too shall soon pass.

Lauren Kenna

Equality Matters

No matter where you are from
equality matters, **we are all equal**, = **we are all one.**
No matter what colour we are,
where we are from, who we are
democracy counts.

We are all born into this world
we will go out into the light of Heaven's door
our actions, our vocabulary, our way of thinking
should be heard in a manner of respect.

Never think ill of anyone.
We are a nation, a world that lives in peace.
We should come together not fight with each other,
listen to each other, share each other's light
and stories with the world.

The pain inflicted
is killing the community.
Its spirit is dying.
Do not let it.

We are all equal, we are all free.
Together only we can stop this hatred.
Only we can stop slavery.
Walls of humanity fall down the darkness

because we are being selfish.
We need to come together.

Leanne Drain

Don't Touch Your Face

Pre-pandemic we just popped down to the shops. Now? We must buy supplies to help us survive these world-shattering times. Plan list so the same spot twice you never visit. In car, tell your PTSD and social anxiety *be quiet!* Enter shops, realising you left your confidence in the boot along with your shopping bags.

Don't touch your face.

In the supermarket, there is a two for one deal on suspicion and fear. Your mission is clear: wipe down trolley, only take what you need. Wear hand sanitiser. Wear a face mask. Wear plastic gloves. Every surface is a weapon, is weaponised: invisible, the virus sleeps. Empty shelves like you've seen in zombie flicks. Ration your panic, because panic has bought everything else. Ain't no pasta, eggs or rice. But look, claustrophobia is now half price. And you could swear *Don't Stand So Close To Me* is playing on repeat: somewhere, a storemanager revels in the irony as a voice comes over the PA: *Just a reminder to customers that social distancing rules are currently in place, and please remember...*

Don't touch your face.

In the toilet paper section, you see an old man staring into the emptiness. Two metres away you ask if he needs any, that you live local, can drop some off from your stash. His smile is grateful. He says *I am merely a tourist, wanted to witness the carnage for myself.* But he thanks you. Profusely. *Kindness is always so expensive in a place like this*, he adds. And there, beneath the fluorescent lights, a tear rolls down your cheek. As you go to brush it away, the old man says:

Don't touch your face.

Don't touch your face.

Don't touch your face.

Scott-Patrick Mitchell

Regenerated Rings

Once it was a dinosaur pine,
light of wood and living,
stretching, leaving
to meet the sun.
Now it lies stone-solid, heaving,
pulling my palm to meet gravity's end.

It had fallen, litter-shrouded, water-logged,
locked in an airless casket.
Rivers cleansed its cellular skeleton
reclaiming decaying matter,
replenishing
silica, pyrite, opal.

I look close to read the regenerated rings
writing a petrified past:
8 million species springing,
80 billion sunsets, daybreaks,
condensing
into a code of colours and contours.

And now – what do the trees still standing
transcribe of our virulent times?
A tale of
black carbon kohl,

plasticine green,
the muted matte of a spring snuffed out?

Will future lines avow our
Anthropocene sins?
Or could this momentary grain be a great resetting -
seeding, rewilding, revealing
whispers of a polychrome paradise.

Vera Zakharov

Night Light

Waterfall of stars at night from man made buildings alight
these unlit hours are going by with cars lighting an ocean
dry breathing life into the darkness tonight and living for
   the nocturnal life alright

it's pitch black but my mind is brighter than the sun, am I
   losing precious sleep to someone?

Curtains up to see the world from above with people up
   doing what they love

others talk about the way we run as if giving up daylight can
   get no one

take the time to read your mind and who knows what you
   might find
a dark place has no end in sight it can allow the quietest to
   shine so bright

works of art and lovers combined help us unleash the idea to
   unwind

for the creative soul working in reverse, feeling as if their
   body is on some kind of curse

let the night take you on a disruptive progress giving you a
   whole new working process

you're not the only one reading this verse thinking, that's
   me whilst taking Night Nurse.

Sammy Dean Monroe

A Dionysian Swell

Out of the blackness
    the darkness
        the bleakness.

Out of the shackles
    the dungeon
        the well.

A sunrise.
A moonbeam.
A nightingale's daydream.
A bag made of moleskins.
The call of the shell.

Out stream the foxes
    the swallows
        the wolf cubs.

Down come the ravens
        the Heathens rebel.

With a spluttering of otherness
a regaining of crazy
a shedding of proper
the wild excel.

And now,
> they sit still-ly.

The wildness,
> they feel truly.

A freedom.
A wonder.
A Dionysian swell.

Heather Joy

Whispers of the Soul

The truth is
that real life begins
when you believe
in what you want.
When pain becomes
a good friend
who helps you
to grow, to be the best.
And maturity is your mountain,
like Everest.
Without regrets
your heart, your soul
become your goal.
The truth is
there is no life,
there is no death,
we are stardust
from the universe
and our journey,
our own mistakes
our quiet tears,
are hard lessons
and also a teacher

to be the best
to love yourself.
And in that moment,
in that day
happiness will be our only way.

Roxana Negut

Left

Left the reason to dress, no one to impress, apart from the dog and you. Comfy, très comfy.
Functional
now I'm punctual!

Left to my own devices, a meeting, smart top, trackie bottoms, doesn't impact on my genius.
Liberation
I never knew I needed.

Left counting countless pinching heels, corresponding clutches, If it itches, digs, or sags ditch it.
Joy
I can survive without it.

Left questioning female conditioning. Realisation I can go bra-less. It's taken so long to acclimatise.
Feel
the enormity of these times.

Left with virtual connections to my inner circle. They had no option but to leave me, tease me.
Kiss
the people I miss.

Left fine dining and the gastro pub for meal planning with the contents of the pulse cupboard.

Plenty
thrill of a takeout curry.

Left to endure endless repeats, reviews, fillers, depressing
　　　news. Indulge in books I never read.
Poems
fall out of my head.

　　　Left wondering what normal is? Essentials I didn't
miss. Stuff
　　　taken I thought were a given.
Live
life is for living.

Vicky Pealing

Lockdown

I walk amid the memory stones
light dappling through verdant green leaves
flickering and fading.

Moving through the past
Beloved mother, treasured son, sorely missed
Edith and Ethel and Clara and Harold and –

crows glide on boot black wings
nested trees dip their arms to embrace
bees hum and suckle.

No sadness, this peaceful place is full of love
it lingers embedded in light and shade
embroidered on the stones.

Remember this when hope seems far away
even in the midst of death
we are in life.

Julie O'Beirne

What's Important Now – 2020

I walk out of the doors and my legs support me.
I smell the air, breathe deeply, feel my lungs expand.
I hear bees hum, soft rustles in the grasses.
I see ants and iridescent beetles.
I taste my coffee and am not nauseated.
I run my fingers through my regrown hair.
Unlike all last year
I have the power to be unremarkable.

Helen Rowlands

Poet Biographies

Helen Cox is a Yorkshire-born novelist and poet. After completing her MA in creative writing at the University of York St. John Helen edited her own independent film magazine for five years and penned three non-fiction books. Her first two novels were published by HarperCollins in 2016. She currently lives by the sea in Sunderland where she writes poetry, romance novellas, and *The Kitt Hartley Yorkshire Mystery Series* alongside hosting The Poetrygram podcast. For more information visit: helencoxbooks.com

Sammy Dean Monroe is a poet and writer who is new to the scene and has a rebellious and comedic style and lyrical style of writing. Originally trained as a dancer and actor, he went from using his body to tell a story to putting pen to paper. Yet still his work has a rhythm and movement influenced by his past. As a member of the lgbtqia+ community much of his writing has a focus on pushing the boundaries and creating conversations about the underrepresented community. You can follow Sammy on Instagram @Sammydeanmonroe.

Leanne Drain has been writing since she was 12 and loves it– it's her passion. She has always enjoyed poetry as it catches her eye. She really enjoys writing as a whole. She has had various pieces published before in *Forward Poetry*. She comes alive when she writes and it fuels her imagination.

Katherine Fitton lives in Cambridge with the plants she keeps on her balcony and always seems to be falling into long distance friendships, but, luckily, travelling to meet them all is one of her greatest pleasures. Administrator in the NHS by day, geek girl and gamer by night, she spends a lot of her time perfecting spreadsheets and organising people. Katherine has enjoyed writing stories all her life, most recently fanfiction, but it wasn't until about a year ago that she turned to poetry, and has found solace in the rhythm and rhyme of it while the world has been in lockdown.

Jacqueline Fowle, now 68, retired from a 38-year career in Kent journalism at the age of 56. Her jobs over the years included reporter, sub-editor, chief sub-editor and editor. She has latterly turned to creative writing, which has included poetry. She enjoys the fellowship of various writing groups and last year was delighted to have a poem published in the Poetrygram Annual 2019. Making it two in a row in 2020 she describes as thrilling. She also enjoys walking, cookery, art and playing bridge. She is married to sports fanatic Roger and has two sons.

Christian Garduno's work can be read in over 40 literary magazines, including *Riza Press*, where his poem, *The Return*, was a Finalist in their 2019 Multimedia Art Contest. He lives and writes in South Texas with his wonderful Nahemie and young son Dylan.

Sharron Green is from Guildford, England and as @rhymes_n_roses on Instagram enjoys sharing her poetry which attempts to make sense of modern life.

Sharron has self-published a book titled *Introducing Rhymes_n_Roses*, and will soon have poems in over ten other international anthologies including two based on the Covid-19 pandemic. She recently relaunched her website: rhymesnroses.com and has started an MA in Creative Writing at the University of Surrey. During 2020 she has found reading, writing and sharing poetry hugely therapeutic and is publishing a booklet of lockdown poems called *Viral Odes* in December.

Born in North-west England, **Heather Joy** is a Person-Centered Experiential Expressive Arts Therapist, PhD student and associate tutor of social sciences. She is a mother of two, novice climber and an emerging poet, with previous and forthcoming publications including: The Poetrygram Annual 2019, Feral, Other Worldly Women's Press, Auroras &Blossoms, Strukturriss, 45 magazine and Nymphs.

Lauren Kenna is an administrator from Manchester, who enjoys writing in her spare time. She has always had a fascination with language and a love of literature, leading her to complete a BA in English and a PGDip in Library and Information Management. You can find more of her work on her Instagram page @whirlwind_of_reveries.

Roxana Negut was born in 1981 in Bucharest, Romania. She studied at the Faculty of Philosophy and Journalism and has worked as an editor, copywriter, content writer and journalist for various publications. She writes children's literature, poetry but also satirical prose. In 2019 she published the book of philosophical poetry *Dead People Don't Want Water* with Lumen Publishing.

In 2020 she published *Shadows of Light* with Lumen Publishing and had poems published in *Chaos, a poetry vortex*, by the Local Gems Poetry Press based in America and in the introspective anthology *Blood Red* Star. Roxana is a member of the Poetry Society of America.

Julie O' Beirne started writing stories and poetry when she was a young girl and had a poem published in Women's Weekly magazine when she was sixteen. Fast forward many years with her children grown and a degree under her belt, Julie started to write again. Last year she won the staff short story competition at the college where she works.

Julie's lockdown poem was inspired by her daily walks around a local cemetery this spring.

Scott-Patrick Mitchell (SPM) is a poet who lives and writes on Whadjuk Noongar Land in Perth, Western Australia. SPM's work appears in *Contemporary Australian Poetry*, *The Fremantle Press Anthology of Western Australian Poetry*, *Solid Air*, *Stories of Perth* and *Going Postal*. In 2019, SPM won Coal Creek's Literary Award for Poetry, The Creative Connections Poetry Prize, Melbourne Poets Union's Martin Downey Urban Realist Poetry Award and The Wollongong Short Story Prize. Most recently, SPM was shortlisted for The International Googie Goer Prize for Speculative Prose and Red Room's 2020 Poetry Fellowship.

Vicky Pealing grew up on a council estate, where she met her husband on a bus. Decades later buses featured again in her commute to work where she manages a children's social work team. She says traffic jams and crowded buses provide her with a creative space. Vicky won first prize in the 2020 Oakwood Literature Festival with *Chad Girl*, a poem about her council estate in the 80s. Vicky's poetry uses imagery and humour to explore these extraordinary times. She loves being with her family, muddy dog walks and video calls with her grandson who lives in Taiwan.

Richard Risemberg was born to a mixed and mixed-up family in Argentina, and dragged to LA as a child to escape the fascist regime. He's spent the next few decades exploring the darker corners of the America Dream and blithering on about it with keyboard or his own big mouth.

He has published widely in the last few years, mostly short fiction in literary journals; you want to see proof? Go to:

crowtreebooks.com/richard-risemberg-publications/ and click a few links. Some of the stories may disturb your sleep; some will give you sweet dreams.

Helen Rowlands is a queer writer, grandma and visual artist who often works across genres, disciplines and definitions. She and her wife live in a beautiful part of South Wales U.K. but have strong family links to Australia which she considers her other home. She lives with cancer and other ongoing health conditions and says that these experiences have impacted much on her recent works including the need to negotiate the changing landscapes of her body and the circumstances of her life. Her poetry often explores both the challenges but also the unexpected joys and gratitude such circumstances can bring.

You can find out more about Helen's work at:

helenrowlandswpp.wix.com.artiste or via Twitter @helen_celtt.

Writing with a decidedly Glaswegian dourness, working class poet and spoken word performer **Greg R Shearer** captures the guttural beauty of life led from below the poverty line. Often autobiographical, his writing details observations of his family, his city and her people wrestling under the weight of their trauma between bittersweet reprieves. You can find more of his work on Instagram @grspoetry.

Tony Simms is a PE teacher and former professional basketballer. He represented England in basketball at every age level including Senior Men's.

Although Tony's life has primarily focused professionally on elite sport, the written word has always had a magnetic draw. It wasn't until he began to write himself that it became embedded into his life. He is a now a prolific writer of poetry and short stories. Tony lives in Birmingham, UK and has two children. He can be found on Twitter @Poetrycathartic and on Instagram: catharticpoetryreal.

Annie Sturgeon is a writer and artist living in Aberdeenshire. Following a degree in Environmental Education, the natural world became the focus of Annie's working and creative life. She currently carries out voluntary surveys for wildlife organisations using her off-road mobility scooter; enabling her to explore less-frequented areas of the countryside at a pace that provides a wealth of inspiration.

Although relatively new to writing, Annie was long-listed for the Ginkgo prize 2019 with two poems. Most recently she has had a short story selected for The Scottish Book Trust 2020 publication, *Future*.

Heather Walker lives in London and writes poetry, flash and short stories. Her work has been published in a number of anthologies including What Was Left (Retreat West) and Stories in Colour (Eylands) as well as Gold Dust magazine, Visual Verse, Paragraph Planet and The People's Friend. She meets regularly with a group of writers in a café by the River Thames and has recently finished writing her first novella in flash.

Richard Westcott, now retired from a happy and fulfilled lifetime of NHS doctoring, no longer has any excuse about not writing poetry. His poems have appeared in all sorts of places like buses, shop windows and on walls, along with more conventional anthologies and magazines – even winning an occasional prize here and there – and his well-received pamphlet is published by Indigo Dreams: indigodreams.co.uk/richard-westcott/4594230918

He blogs at: richardwestcottspoetry.com

Vera Zakharov is a Russian-American living in Brighton with her partner, toddler and cat. For work and vocation she campaigns on food issues with a national food charity. For soulful nourishment she forages, wild swims, star-gazes and explores beautiful British landscapes with her family. She is particularly keen on ancient monuments, dismantled railways, and myths connected with nature and the seasons. She is an occasional amateur writer of poems and short essays, when work and parenting allows.

Tune into The Poetrygram Podcast at:
helencoxbooks.com/podcasts

www.ingramcontent.com/pod-product-compliance
Lightning Source LLC
Chambersburg PA
CBHW021452080526
44588CB00009B/821